teacher PLANNER

THIS PLANNER BELONGS TO:

_____

Want free goodies?!

Email us at

prettysimplebooks@gmail.com

Title the email "Prepare to be Schooled!" and let us know that you purchased a Pretty Simple Planner!

Find us on Instagram!

@prettysimplebooks

Questions & Customer Service:
Email us at prettysimplebooks@gmail.com!

Teacher Planner Lesson Planner
©Pretty Simple Planners. All rights reserved. No part of this publication may be reproduced, distributed, or transmitted, in any form or by any means, including photocopying, recording, or other mechanical methods, without prior written permission of the publisher, except in the case of brief quotations embodied in critical reviews and certain other noncommercial uses permitted by copyright law.

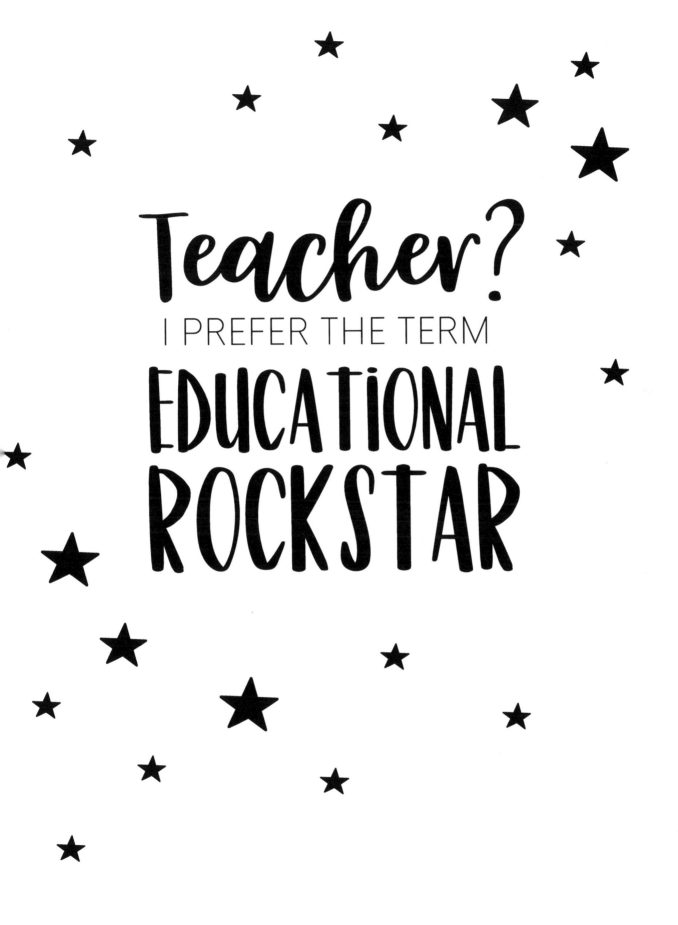

IMPORTANT DATES

January
NEW YEAR'S DAY
MARTIN LUTHER KING DAY

February
GROUNDHOG DAY
VALENTINE'S DAY
PRESIDENTS DAY

March
ST. PATRICK'S DAY

July
INDEPENDENCE DAY

August

September
LABOR DAY

April

APRIL FOOL'S DAY
EARTH DAY

May

CINCO DE MAYO
MOTHER'S DAY
MEMORIAL DAY

June

FATHER'S DAY

October

COLUMBUS DAY
HALLOWEEN

November

VETERANS DAY
THANKSGIVING

December

HANUKKAH
CHRISTMAS EVE
CHRISTMAS DAY
NEW YEAR'S EVE

July 2022

SUNDAY	MONDAY	TUESDAY	WEDNESDAY
3	4 **INDEPENDENCE DAY**	5	6
10	11	12	13
17	18	19	20
National Ice Cream Day 24 / 31	25	26	27

[Live in the sunshine, swim the sea and drink the wild air.
— Ralph Waldo Emerson]

THURSDAY	FRIDAY	SATURDAY	NOTES
	1	2	
7	8	9	
14	15	16	
21	22	23	
28	29	30	

WEEK OF _____	Monday	Tuesday
SUBJECT:		

Wednesday	Thursday	Friday

WEEK OF _____	Monday	Tuesday
SUBJECT:		

Wednesday	Thursday	Friday

WEEK OF _____	Monday	Tuesday
SUBJECT:		

Wednesday	Thursday	Friday

WEEK OF _____	Monday	Tuesday
SUBJECT:		

Wednesday	Thursday	Friday

WEEK OF _____	Monday	Tuesday
SUBJECT:		

Wednesday	Thursday	Friday

August 2022

SUNDAY	MONDAY	TUESDAY	WEDNESDAY
	1	2	3
7	8	9 *Book Lovers Day*	10
14	15	16 *Tell a Joke Day*	17
21	22	23	24
28	29	30	31

[The secret of getting ahead is getting started.
— Mark Twain]

THURSDAY	FRIDAY	SATURDAY	NOTES
4	5	6	
11	12	13	
18	19	20	
25	26 *National Dog Day*	27	

WEEK OF _____	Monday	Tuesday
SUBJECT:		

Wednesday	Thursday	Friday

WEEK OF _____	Monday	Tuesday
SUBJECT:		

Wednesday	Thursday	Friday

WEEK OF _____	Monday	Tuesday
SUBJECT:		

Wednesday	Thursday	Friday

WEEK OF _____	Monday	Tuesday
SUBJECT:		

Wednesday	Thursday	Friday

WEEK OF _____	Monday	Tuesday
SUBJECT:		

Wednesday	Thursday	Friday

September 2022

SUNDAY	MONDAY	TUESDAY	WEDNESDAY
4	5 **LABOR DAY**	6	7
11	12	13	14
18	19	20	21 *World Gratitude Day*
25	26 **ROSH HASHANAH**	27	28

> Life is something that everyone should try at least once.
> – Henry J. Tillman

THURSDAY	FRIDAY	SATURDAY
1	2	3
8	9	10
15	16	17
22	23	24
29	30	

NOTES

WEEK OF _____	Monday	Tuesday
SUBJECT:		

Wednesday	Thursday	Friday

WEEK OF _____	Monday	Tuesday
SUBJECT:		

Wednesday	Thursday	Friday

WEEK OF _____	Monday	Tuesday
SUBJECT:		

Wednesday	Thursday	Friday

WEEK OF _____	Monday	Tuesday
SUBJECT:		

Wednesday	Thursday	Friday

WEEK OF _____	Monday	Tuesday
SUBJECT:		

Wednesday	Thursday	Friday

October 2022

SUNDAY	MONDAY	TUESDAY	WEDNESDAY
2	3	4 *National Taco Day*	5 YOM KIPPUR
9	10 INDIGENOUS PEOPLES' DAY	11	12
16	17	18	19
23 / 30	24 / 31 HALLOWEEN	25	26

[I am not afraid; I was born to do this.
- Joan of Arc]

THURSDAY	FRIDAY	SATURDAY	NOTES
		1	
6	7 *World Smile Day*	8	
13	14	15	
20	21	22	
27	28	29	

WEEK OF _____	Monday	Tuesday
SUBJECT:		

Wednesday	Thursday	Friday

WEEK OF _____	Monday	Tuesday
SUBJECT:		

Wednesday	Thursday	Friday

WEEK OF _____	Monday	Tuesday
SUBJECT:		

Wednesday	Thursday	Friday

WEEK OF _____	Monday	Tuesday
SUBJECT:		

Wednesday	Thursday	Friday

WEEK OF _____	Monday	Tuesday
SUBJECT:		

Wednesday	Thursday	Friday

November 2022

SUNDAY	MONDAY	TUESDAY	WEDNESDAY
		1	2
6 DAYLIGHT SAVINGS ENDS	7	8	9
13 World Kindness Day	14	15	16
20	21	22	23
27	28	29	30

> True happiness is to enjoy the present, without anxious dependence on the future.
> – Seneca

THURSDAY	FRIDAY	SATURDAY
3	4	5
10	11 VETERANS DAY	12
17	18	19
24 THANKSGIVING	25	26

NOTES

WEEK OF _____

SUBJECT:

	Monday	Tuesday

Wednesday	Thursday	Friday

WEEK OF _____	Monday	Tuesday
SUBJECT:		

Wednesday	Thursday	Friday

WEEK OF _____	Monday	Tuesday
SUBJECT:		

Wednesday	Thursday	Friday

WEEK OF _____	Monday	Tuesday
SUBJECT:		

Wednesday	Thursday	Friday

WEEK OF _____	Monday	Tuesday
SUBJECT:		

Wednesday	Thursday	Friday

December 2022

SUNDAY	MONDAY	TUESDAY	WEDNESDAY
4	5	6	7
11	12	13	14
18 HANUKKAH	19	20	21
25 CHRISTMAS DAY	26 KWANZAA	27	28

> [The good we do today becomes the happiness of tomorrow.
> — William James]

THURSDAY	FRIDAY	SATURDAY
1	2	3
8	9	10
15	16	17
22	23	24 CHRISTMAS EVE
29	30	31 NEW YEAR'S EVE

NOTES

WEEK OF _____	Monday	Tuesday
SUBJECT:		

Wednesday	Thursday	Friday

WEEK OF _____	Monday	Tuesday
SUBJECT:		

Wednesday	Thursday	Friday

WEEK OF _____	Monday	Tuesday
SUBJECT:		

Wednesday	Thursday	Friday

WEEK OF _____	Monday	Tuesday
SUBJECT:		

Wednesday	Thursday	Friday

WEEK OF _____	Monday	Tuesday
SUBJECT:		

Wednesday	Thursday	Friday

January 2023

SUNDAY	MONDAY	TUESDAY	WEDNESDAY
1 NEW YEAR'S DAY	2	3	4
8	9	10	11
15	16 MARTIN LUTHER KING JR. DAY	17	18
22	23	24	25
29	30	31	

> If your actions inspire others to dream more, learn more, do more and become more, you are a leader. — John Quincy Adams

THURSDAY	FRIDAY	SATURDAY	NOTES
5	6	7	
12	13	14	
19 *National Popcorn Day*	20	21	
26	27	28	

WEEK OF _____	Monday	Tuesday
SUBJECT:		

Wednesday	Thursday	Friday

WEEK OF _____	Monday	Tuesday
SUBJECT:		

Wednesday	Thursday	Friday

WEEK OF _____	Monday	Tuesday
SUBJECT:		

Wednesday	Thursday	Friday

WEEK OF _____	Monday	Tuesday
SUBJECT:		

Wednesday	Thursday	Friday

WEEK OF _____	Monday	Tuesday
SUBJECT:		

Wednesday	Thursday	Friday

february 2023

SUNDAY	MONDAY	TUESDAY	WEDNESDAY
			1
5	6	7	8
12	13	14 VALENTINE'S DAY	15
19	20 PRESIDENTS' DAY	21	22
26	27	28	

> [Love inspires, illuminates, designates, and leads the way.
> — Mary Baker Eddy]

THURSDAY	FRIDAY	SATURDAY	NOTES
2	3	4	
9	10	11 *Make a Friend Day*	
16	17	18	
23	24	25	

WEEK OF _____	Monday	Tuesday
SUBJECT:		

Wednesday	Thursday	Friday

WEEK OF _____	Monday	Tuesday
SUBJECT:		

Wednesday	Thursday	Friday

WEEK OF _____	Monday	Tuesday
SUBJECT:		

Wednesday	Thursday	Friday

WEEK OF _____	Monday	Tuesday
SUBJECT:		

Wednesday	Thursday	Friday

WEEK OF _____	Monday	Tuesday
SUBJECT:		

Wednesday	Thursday	Friday

March 2023

SUNDAY	MONDAY	TUESDAY	WEDNESDAY
			1
5	6	7	8
12 *DAYLIGHT SAVINGS BEGINS*	13	14 *National Pi Day*	15
19	20	21	22
26	27	28	29

[One of the first signs of a spirit-filled life is enthusiasm.
— A.B. Simpson]

THURSDAY	FRIDAY	SATURDAY
2	3	4
9	10	11
16	17 ST. PATRICK'S DAY	18
23	24	25
30	31	

NOTES

WEEK OF _____	Monday	Tuesday
SUBJECT:		

Wednesday	Thursday	Friday

WEEK OF _____	Monday	Tuesday
SUBJECT:		

Wednesday	Thursday	Friday

WEEK OF _____	Monday	Tuesday
SUBJECT:		

Wednesday	Thursday	Friday

WEEK OF _____	Monday	Tuesday
SUBJECT:		

Wednesday	Thursday	Friday

WEEK OF _____	Monday	Tuesday
SUBJECT:		

Wednesday	Thursday	Friday

April 2023

SUNDAY	MONDAY	TUESDAY	WEDNESDAY
2	3	4	5
9 *EASTER*	10 *National Siblings Day*	11	12
16	17	18	19
23 / 30	24	25	26

> In the small matters trust the mind, the large ones the heart.
> – Sigmund Freud

THURSDAY	FRIDAY	SATURDAY	NOTES
		1	
6	7 *GOOD FRIDAY*	8	
13	14	15	
20	21	22 *EARTH DAY*	
27	28	29	

WEEK OF _____	Monday	Tuesday
SUBJECT:		

Wednesday	Thursday	Friday

WEEK OF _____	Monday	Tuesday
SUBJECT:		

Wednesday	Thursday	Friday

WEEK OF _____	Monday	Tuesday
SUBJECT:		

Wednesday	Thursday	Friday

WEEK OF _____	Monday	Tuesday
SUBJECT:		

Wednesday	Thursday	Friday

WEEK OF _____	Monday	Tuesday
SUBJECT:		

Wednesday	Thursday	Friday

May 2023

SUNDAY	MONDAY	TUESDAY	WEDNESDAY
	1	2	3
7	8	9	10
14 MOTHER'S DAY	15	16	17
21	22	23	24
28	29 MEMORIAL DAY	30	31

> For success, attitude is equally as important as ability.
> – Walter Scott

THURSDAY	FRIDAY	SATURDAY	NOTES
4	5 *Cinco de Mayo*	6	
11	12	13	
18	19	20	
25	26	27	

WEEK OF _____	Monday	Tuesday
SUBJECT:		

Wednesday	Thursday	Friday

WEEK OF _____	Monday	Tuesday
SUBJECT:		

Wednesday	Thursday	Friday

WEEK OF _____

SUBJECT:

Monday

Tuesday

Wednesday	Thursday	Friday

WEEK OF _____	Monday	Tuesday
SUBJECT:		

Wednesday	Thursday	Friday

WEEK OF _____	Monday	Tuesday
SUBJECT:		

Wednesday	Thursday	Friday

June 2023

SUNDAY	MONDAY	TUESDAY	WEDNESDAY
4	5	6	7
11	12	13	14
18 FATHER'S DAY	19 JUNETEENTH	20	21 World Music Day
25	26	27	28

Flag Day (14)

[Adventure is worthwhile in itself.
- Amelia Earhart]

THURSDAY	FRIDAY	SATURDAY	NOTES
1	2 *National Donut Day*	3	
8	9	10	
15	16	17	
22	23	24	
29	30		

WEEK OF _____	Monday	Tuesday
SUBJECT:		

Wednesday	Thursday	Friday

WEEK OF _____	Monday	Tuesday
SUBJECT:		

Wednesday	Thursday	Friday

WEEK OF _____	Monday	Tuesday
SUBJECT:		

Wednesday	Thursday	Friday

WEEK OF _____	Monday	Tuesday
SUBJECT:		

Wednesday	Thursday	Friday

WEEK OF _____	Monday	Tuesday
SUBJECT:		

Wednesday	Thursday	Friday

STUDENT BIRTHDAYS

January	February	March

July	August	September

April	May	June

October	November	December

ATTENDANCE OR GRADE TRACKER

ATTENDANCE OR GRADE TRACKER

ATTENDANCE OR GRADE TRACKER

Made in United States
Orlando, FL
27 July 2022